BUILDING CHARACTER

The Values Journal

STEVEN R. JOHNSON

ISBN 978-1-64349-099-1 (paperback)
ISBN 978-1-64349-100-4 (digital)

Christian Faith Publishing, Inc.
832 Park Avenue
Meadville, PA 16335
www.christianfaithpublishing.com

Scripture quotations taken from the Holy Bible, New International Version (NIV) © 1973, 1978, 1984, 2011 by Biblica Inc. Used by permission. All rights reserved.

Printed in the United States of America

Contents

Preface

Late one night, after putting my kids to bed and lying down to try to fall asleep, it occurred to me that over the course of my life, I have read many books on philosophy, leadership, and character; but I have not seen a lot of good examples that focus attention on teaching children the underlying values that support character development. Both of my kids are naturally curious and constantly seek answers to difficult questions that I have to really consider before providing an answer. As much as I love these opportunities to explain my knowledge of how the world works, I feel that the experience of discovering your own answers leads to deeper understanding. This journal is designed to aid kids in the journey of discovery as they seek deep understanding of what it means to live a life based on core values and develop their own character that will last a lifetime.

This does not take away from our responsibility as parents to support and guide our kids throughout their lives. We as parents must internalize these values and provide the example to our children to make it easier for them to follow the same path. Live your values every day, and good character will flow naturally from your habits.

Acknowledgments

I need to say a special thank-you to my wife, who continues to inspire me every day to be a better husband, father, and man. Without her, it would not be possible to accomplish our family's goals. She is the driving force behind our family, and I love her with all my heart.

Based on my experience, God puts special people in our lives, and we should learn to recognize them and hold on tight. In the spirit of this journal, it should be noted that it is extremely important to have people in your life that represent the values you wish to live. Learn from them. Share with them. Love them.

Introduction for Parents

The cultural norms present in today's society are different than those of previous generations. Trends throughout history have demonstrated cultural shifts over time, but the pace of change has accelerated in more recent history. Changes in the way we communicate, travel and engage in economic activity have had a direct impact on these accelerated changes.

Just think that within the past thirty years, mail has changed from a letter that had to be physically transported across a geographic distance over a period of days to digital communication, through e-mail that occurs near instantaneously. Person-to-person communication used to be restricted to those times and places where people could gather or when they had access to a telephone that was connected to a hardline. Now cell phone use is nearly universal, and communication can take place without regard to geographic limitations. The proliferation of air travel has made international travel accessible to almost all societal classes around the globe. Globalization's impact on production supply chains allows goods to be produced in one place, assembled in another, and delivered to consumers in a totally different market. All these rapid changes have impacted the way we interact with one another and our expectations for our immediate societal environment.

While cultural norms previously adjusted slowly to our changing environment, norms today struggle to keep pace with our changing world. The result of this discrepancy is a confused cultural identity that is not rooted in a solid foundation of values and reflected in previous generations' unshakable character. The symptoms of this change are visible in our daily lives, surrounded by the constant desire for immediate gratification. Focus on community is shifting toward the self, resulting in a more selfish, egotistical, and narcissistic society. This trend can be confronted and overcome, but it requires the hard work and dedication of parents to raise kids that develop strong character rooted in core values. This is a call to action, and this journal is designed to serve as a guide to start your journey.

The idea of this journal is to establish a framework for engagement and communication with your children while creating a tool for your children to use to focus on character development through the deliberate practice of core values. Your children are provided with broad references to values, allowing them to explore the meaning of each value for themselves. This exploration will support a deeper understanding of each value and ultimately aid in the internalization of these values to build character. The space to provide a definition is a critical first step to this process. Parents, you will have to do your homework so that you can have a constructive discussion with your children to support their definition development.

Dictionary definitions of words are often difficult for kids to understand, unless the words are presented in context. This is your job. Create context for each value by explaining it to you children. Use stories as often as possible and make it personal and relatable. Discuss your experiences or relay stories of value exemplification you have encountered during your lifetime. Share stories about your family or close friends to bring your circle closer together. And always remember that your children are vigilant observers. Exemplify the behavior you want them to emulate. Trust me, they are watching and constantly learning.

Empower Your Children

One of the core principles in this journal is for parents to empower their children to make values-based decisions. For your children to create the experiences necessary for them to practice values and build habits, you as parents must grant them the freedom and opportunity to do so. This comes from empowerment. You must ensure that your children understand that with this freedom to decide comes a great deal of responsibility to act in a way that is consistent with the values they are learning. Remind them that in life, decisions we make have consequences. The types of consequences depend on the wisdom we apply when deciding.

Eventually, your children will also face moral dilemmas. This is when the options on both sides of the decision require applying specific values, but with contradictory results. In these instances, good judgment and wisdom will guide their decision. An example might be when your children are faced with the decision to risk friendship, and the trust that binds it, because a friend is acting in a manner inconsistent with other values. This might be something as simple as a friend acting out in class or as difficult as a friend involved in something illegal. It is your responsibility to equip them with the decision-making skills to face these types of conflicts. And you should remember that when your children own the decision, they will be far more invested in the outcome and the consequences.

At the heart of this concept of empowerment is the idea that our children will make informed decisions based significantly on the knowledge we impart. This is where your example is critical. You provide the context for their decisions by demonstrating your values in the decisions you make every day. Communicating examples of your personal experience will help your children internalize their values. This will create shared values within your household, and you will realize your success when your children make independent choices and you say to yourself, *That is what I would have done.*

Smart Empowerment

Give your children the tools they need to make the right decisions at the right time, and you will achieve smart empowerment. By smart empowerment, I mean allow your children the space and opportunity to make their own decisions, but do so in a way that promotes learning. This does not mean that they have to be successful at everything they do. We can learn a lot from our failures too. It does mean that you are responsible for guiding them through their decisions, when necessary, and providing support and understanding when the time is right. Smart empowerment does not mean you let your children do whatever they want and deal with the consequences. It does mean you have a responsibility to help them avoid impossible situations that they are not equipped to handle. When you find the right balance between guiding and letting go for your child, you will fully understand what smart empowerment is. The results of smart empowerment will be the rapid internalization of values and an enduring character for your children.

This journal provides you with a tool to execute smart empowerment in a methodical way that creates lasting effects. The journal provides the focus for your opportunity to communicate with your children. The structure of the journal allows you to start off each day with guidance and focus while ending each day with reflection and learning. As a tool, it will allow you the opportunity to explore the choices your children face and the actions they decide to take. It is often difficult to get your children to articulate the events of their day, but this journal will help you to gain a deeper understanding of the type of person they are developing into.

Your Responsibility

It is your responsibility to keep the lines of communication open with your children to allow growth to occur. Your communication environment must allow for the free flow of ideas in both directions and cannot become your personal soapbox. Your children will not learn as much and grow as rapidly if they are subjected to lectures. The question format of the journal is designed for you to be able to engage the topic and listen to your children's ideas. You should also ask follow-on questions to get deeper into the topics depending on where the conversation takes you. Remember to set aside enough time for this to occur because you don't want this time to be cut short due to competing priorities.

Prepare

Parents, for this effort to be as successful as possible, you will have to do your homework. It is important for you to be able to clearly express your understanding of each of the values in this journal in a way that your children can understand them. Don't worry, this section is designed to help you do just that.

Definitions

In my experience, the path to understanding each value begins with defining the value in simple terms. What follows are my definitions of each value for you to use as tools as you develop your own.

Humility—acting in a way that shows your ability to do things well without flaunting your success.

Work—applying effort toward a task in order to complete it.

Discipline—consistently working toward your goals with determination. (Determination is your commitment to action.)

Trust—a relationship with another person in which you believe the other person will act in a reasonable and responsible way.

Faith—believing in something wholeheartedly without the need for physical evidence.

Liberty—the freedom to act without the fear of unreasonable reaction.

Perseverance—not giving up even when you are facing a difficult situation.

Love—caring for someone so deeply that you are prepared to do almost anything for them. (It is important to distinguish between the love for one another and your love for God. Love between people must be expressed as "almost anything" because your love for another should not—and must not—justify breaking God's laws.)

Resilience—being able to recover from setbacks or challenges.

Service—doing work for the benefit of others.

Prudence—making decisions based on understanding and experience.

Practice—seeking the best way to do something and repeating it in order to achieve perfect execution.

Courtesy—demonstrating respect for others by acting the way you would want others to act toward you.

Gratitude—being thankful for what has been provided to or for you.

Respect—treating others fairly.

Concentration/focus—applying your attention on an effort or toward an action without distraction.

Patience—being willing to wait for results and acting with understanding toward others.

Generosity—giving without consideration for payment, recognition, or reward.

Honesty/integrity—acting and communicating truthfully. Doing what you say you are going to do.

Justice—fair treatment and acting in a way that is consistent with established rules and laws.

Courage—acting even when you are afraid to do something. Facing your fears.

Kindness—being nice and polite to others.

Responsibility—owning your actions in a way in which you accept the results and the consequences.

Tolerance—accepting others for who they are.

Empathy—showing that you understand the way others feel in a particular situation.

Compassion—caring for others.

Loyalty—commitment to ideas or other people.

Friendship—committing to share time and experiences with another person through a mutual relationship.

Self-control—acting or not acting in a way that is consistent with your values. (This eventually leads to a demonstration of your character.)

Mercy—demonstrating kindness when you are in a position of control.

Contentedness—being happy or satisfied with your identity, position, or possessions.

*****

This introduction has been written to help you prepare yourself to serve as a guide for your child as they learn to become the best person he can be. The environment in which our children are growing up is proving to be complex, interconnected, and fast-paced. We must prepare our children to face this environment with a clear understanding of who they are and what it means to demonstrate their character through their actions and words. I think the best advice I can offer you is to be prepared. Think through how you intend to explain each value before you engage your child. Use the definitions available or write your own in a way that you can best explain each value. Be familiar with the stories you will share with your child and expect to answer questions. And most of all, take it one step at a time. You are their guide on a lifelong journey of learning and discovery. Always be available, and be prepared for anything.

Introduction for Kids

Kids, your parents have their own introduction section, so it is only fair that you have one written specifically for you. I want you to enjoy following the development of character throughout your life. It is within you to be the kind of person you want to be. So you will have to decide what type of person that is. As you go about your day, you will find opportunities to show what kind of person you are or want to be, by the way you act and the way you treat other people. At some point in your life, somebody has probably told you about the golden rule: treat other people the same way you want them to treat you. This idea, if everyone followed it, would make our world a different and friendlier place. It is up to you to act in the best way possible so you can do your part to make the world a better place.

This journal is designed for you. It was made to help you understand values that will lead you on a path toward good character. The goal is for you to explore each of the thirty-one values in your own way. You will be able to write your own definitions and answer key questions about how you experienced each value. There is also a space for you to draw or write anything else you would like.

Don't worry if you don't understand the meaning of each value right away. You will uncover the true meaning of each value in your own way through your own experiences. For your parents, I highlighted the need for them to act as your guide through this process. That will require them to focus their attention on preparing, listening to, and providing you with feedback on your journey. You will have to commit to act in a way that allows you to experience growth through the practice of your values in your words and your actions.

Remember to be patient as you go through this process. You are going to make mistakes, you are going to experience consequences, and you are going to have to ask for help at times. But it is important for you to challenge yourself so that you can truly grow. In the following section, you will find the principles behind this journal. Whenever you need a reminder, go back and read them again. Now it is time for you to commit to understand each value as completely as possible. Talk about values with your family and friends to reinforce your learning. Most of all, learn as much as you can from those that have gone before you.

The Principles of This Journal

This journal is structured around four principles to support your character development. Each principle represents a critical step to lifelong learning and development. Mastering these principles will help you to achieve results in anything you decide to pursue. Keep these principles in mind every day as you focus on your values. They will support you in your commitment to action.

Discipline

You must be dedicated to working hard and committed to practicing your values to be successful. Discipline is a value that underpins all the other values and can be described as the drive that allows you to consistently commit to action. Through the exercise of discipline, you will be able to practice your values systematically even if your motivation begins to fade. Through discipline, you will make your personal commitment to act a priority above other activities everyday and achieve your goals. When you have the ability to act in a disciplined manner, you will be able to take small, incremental steps over time to arrive at long-term goals. This includes activities such as committing to practice a sport to be able to play at a high level of skill; practicing an instrument to perform musical masterpieces; and learning a new skill through the process of trial and error. The achievement of long-term goals results in a feeling of deep satisfaction and fulfillment that can only be achieved through deliberate practice enabled by a commitment to discipline.

Practice

The core principle of this book is development through practice. Practice is driven by the attention and focus used when executing tasks to continuously repeat them while trying to develop perfect execution.

Put simply, if you want to be good at something, you have to repeat it many times so you can find the best way to do it. Once you have found the best way to do it you must continue to practice doing it so it becomes something that you can do naturally.

When seeking to develop the character you wish to demonstrate in your life, it is important to focus your attention on practicing the specific behaviors that exemplify that character. The process of practice leads, over time, to the development of habits that will become natural actions. Your habits will be a clear demonstration of your dedication to practice. Habits are those actions that are executed without the need for deep thought or planning. Throughout your life, the habits that you develop will build into a strong character that is the foundation of living a good and virtuous life.

Challenge Yourself

In addition to practice, you must step out of your normal day-to-day activities to effect real change in your life. Following consistent routines can help you maintain stability in your life, but seeking opportunities to take risks will allow growth to occur. There are different types of risk, and they are appropriate at different times in your life.

For the purposes of this journal, the intent of taking risks is to help you find opportunities to practice and demonstrate your values by taking actions that you would not normally take. These actions may seem small at times, like saying "Thank you" consistently when trying to demonstrate gratitude; but when they are done consistently, they create huge, lasting change.

Your first challenge is to listen closely to your parents and describe the things that they most often repeat when they are asking you to do something. Consider these things challenges that you should seek to confront and overcome. It could be something like cleaning your room or putting things away when you are finished with them, learning not to interrupt others' conversations, saying "Please" when asking or saying "Thank you" when receiving, focusing on the task in front of you instead of giving in to distractions; being kind to others, sharing, etc. Seek small challenges daily, and you will find long-term results.

Seek Wisdom

> By wisdom a house is built, and through understanding it is established; through knowledge its rooms are filled with rare and beautiful treasures. (Prov. 24:3–4)

Wisdom is rooted in the thoughts and actions that have proven their strength over and over again. Seek knowledge by absorbing as much information as you can. Spend time reading to explore what others have already discovered. Not only can wisdom be found throughout history, it can also be found in those around us that have lived different experiences and can share their unique perspective. Ask a lot of questions, but remember it is important that when you have the opportunity to listen, you do so intently.

> Pay attention and turn your ear to the sayings of the wise. (Prov. 22:17)

Focus your energy on gaining knowledge, and when you couple your knowledge with experience, you will develop wisdom. Throughout this journal, you will have the opportunity to read bits of information to increase your knowledge, but it is up to you to commit to action and gain experience. This journal will help you to write down your actions so that you can reflect on them. Reflection will allow you to determine which actions represent the kind of person you want to be and which ones do not. This will shape the choices you make in the future when faced with similar situations. Making good choices about your actions based on previous decisions leads to experience. Now pair these experiences with your knowledge to develop wisdom.

Historical References

Don't feel as though you are alone. Many people throughout history have had to confront challenges and find solutions. Parents, you should talk to your kids about historical figures and explain what made these individuals so remarkable. This section is designed to give you a starting point. Find your own examples in history that demonstrate the type of person you want to grow to be.

Establishing a nation founded on the principle of shared values and common morals was at the forefront of the Founding Fathers' minds during the formation of the United States. In order for a society to function properly, there must be shared culture that is rooted in common values. This idea is rooted in the need for the population to be knowledgeable and educated. The following passages highlight some of this thinking and provide the historical context for the need to learn early in life the values that drive character development and lead to responsible citizenship.

George Washington

As General George Washington prepared the Continental Army for the Battle of Long Island, he gave an address on Tuesday, August 27,

1776. What follows is an excerpt from that address. In that address, General Washington makes clear his conviction to act on behalf of an emerging nation to seek freedom from tyranny.

> The time is now near at hand which must probably determine whether Americans are to be freemen or slaves . . . The fate of unborn millions will now depend, under God, on the courage and conduct of this army. Our cruel and unrelenting enemy leaves us no choice but a brave resistance, or the most abject submission; this is all we can expect. We have therefore to resolve to conquer or die . . .

George Washington's commitment and personal sacrifice was done because he was attached to a cause that was bigger than any one man. He saw in this cause, justice and liberty for men that was to be epitomized by the men who fought for it. And of course, he recognized God's role in realizing the cause of America.

> Let us therefore rely upon the goodness of the cause, and aid of the Supreme Being, in whose hands victory is, to animate and encourage us to great and noble actions. The eyes of all our countrymen are now upon us, and we shall have their blessings and praises, if happily we are the instruments of saving them from the tyranny mediated against them. Let us therefore . . . show the whole world that a freeman contending for liberty on his own ground is superior to any slavish mercenary on earth. (George Washington, General Orders, July 2, 1776)

George Washington's Farewell Address of 1796 provides a prime example of his expectations for this still-young nation. Washington notes that the key to the success of a representative government lies in its collective morality defined by the unification of individual values.

> Of all the depositions and habits which lead to political prosperity, religion and morality are indispensable supports. In vain would that man claim the tribute of patriotism, who should labor to subvert these great pillars of human happiness, these firmest props of the duties of men and citizens . . .
> It is substantially true that virtue or morality is a necessary spring of popular government. The rule, indeed, extends with more or less force to every species of free government.

Washington also points out the need for the population to be knowledgeable in order to contribute effectively to society through the representative government.

> Promote then, as an object of primary importance, institutions for the general diffusion of knowledge. In proportion as the structure of a government gives force to public opinion, it is essential that public opinion should be enlightened.

John Adams and Abigail Adams

John and Abigail Adams note the importance of character represented in the outward display of values in messages to the generations coming up behind them.

John Adams

In a letter to his granddaughter Caroline Amelia Smith De Windt, Adams describes the effects of experience and knowledge accrued over a lifetime. Adams highlights that a lifetime of inquiry leads to more inquiry. But Adams goes on to instruct that his granddaughter should live the core values of love, mercy, and humility throughout her life.

> You are not singular in your suspicions that you know but a little. The longer I live, the more I read, the more patiently I think, and the more anxiously I inquire, the less I seem to know . . . Do justly. Love Mercy. Walk humbly. This is enough . . . So questions and so answers your affectionate grandfather.

In this quote, it appears that John Adams was paraphrasing Micah 6:8, which says, "He has shown you, humankind, what is good! What does the Divine request of you but to do justice, to love kindness, and to walk humbly with your Lord?"

John Adams, throughout his political career, made known the importance of religion and morality to achieve and sustain freedom. This line of thinking is clear in the following series of quotes:

> Religion and morality alone, which can establish the principles upon which freedom can securely stand. The only foundation of a free constitution is pure virtue (1776).
>
> Religion and virtue are the only foundations, not only of republicanism and of all free government, but of social felicity under all governments and in all the combinations of human society. (Letter to Benjamin Rush, 1811)
>
> Without national morality a republican government cannot be maintained. (Letter to Benjamin Rush, February 2, 1807)

John Adams also describes that a government, which is responsible for such a complex mixture of people and territory, must itself exemplify the values epitomized by Moses, Job, Solomon, and Daniel.

> The Management of so complicated and mighty a Machine, as the United Colonies, requires the Meekness of Moses, the Patience of Job and the Wisdom of Solomon, added to the Valor of Daniel. (Letter to James Warren, April 1776)

Abigail Adams

Abigail Adams expresses her sentiment in regard to values when she writes to her son John Quincy Adams as he departs for a journey across the Atlantic Ocean with his father, John Adams.

> The habits of a vigorous mind are formed in contending with difficulties. All history will convince you of this, and that wisdom and penetration are the fruit of experience, not the lessons of retirement and leisure. Great necessities call out great virtues. When a mind is raised and animated by scenes that engage the heart, then those qualities, which would otherwise lie dormant, wake into life and form the character of the hero and the statesman.

Benjamin Franklin

In his speech before the Constitutional Convention on June 28, 1787, Benjamin Franklin expressed the need to recognize God's role in the creation of the United States. This speech was Benjamin Franklin's call for daily prayer before starting the proceedings of the Constitutional Convention.

> I have lived, Sir, a long time and the longer I live, the more convincing proofs I see of this truth

- that God governs in the affairs of men. And if a sparrow cannot fall to the ground without His notice, is it probable that an empire can rise without his aid?

Alexander Hamilton

In Federalist Paper No. 15, Alexander Hamilton highlights the need for government. Once the struggle for independence was complete, the work to create a united nation began. This work is rooted in the need for government.

> Why has government been instituted at all? Because the passions of men will not conform to the dictates of reason and justice without constraint?

Calvin Coolidge

Calvin Coolidge correctly noted that at the base of American culture, which is ultimately reflected in the government, there is a foundation built on the values in the Bible. Directly tied to this underlying foundation is the faith it takes to apply these teachings every day.

> The foundation of our society and our government rest so much on the teachings of the Bible that it would be difficult to support them if faith in these teachings would cease to be practically universal in our country.

James Madison

James Madison points out that each person has a natural right to pursue his personal religious convictions. He also stresses that religious freedom is not merely a right among men but that the expression of religion is one's duty to God.

> The religion of every man must be left to the conviction and conscience of every man; and it is the right of every man to exercise it as these may dictate. This right is in its nature an unalienable right. It is unalienable, because the opinions of men, depending only on the evidence contemplated by their minds cannot follow the dictates of other men; It is unalienable also, because what is here a right toward men, is a duty toward the Creator. It is the duty of every man to render to the Creator such homage and such only as he believes to be acceptable to him. This duty is precedent, both in order of time and in degree of obligation, to the claims of civil society. Before any man can be considered as a member of civil society, he must be considered as a subject of the Governor of the Universe. (Remonstrance against Religious Assessments, June 20, 1785).

Jedidiah Morse and Daniel Webster

Despite the clear conviction of the overwhelming influence religion played in the foundation of the United States, Jedidiah Morse and Daniel Webster recognized the danger in losing this connection.

Jedidiah Morse

> Our dangers are of two kinds, those which affect our religion, and those which affect our government. They are, however, so closely allied that they cannot, with propriety, be separated . . . To the kindly influence of Christianity we owe that

degree of civil freedom, and political and social happiness . . . mankind now enjoys. In proportion as the genuine effects of Christianity are diminished in any nation . . . in the same proportion will the people of that nation recede from the blessings of genuine freedom . . . It follows, that all efforts made to destroy the foundations of our holy religion, ultimately tend to the subversion also of our political freedom and happiness. Whenever the pillars of Christianity shall be overthrown, our present republican forms of government, and all the blessings which flow from them, must fall with them. (1799 sermon)

Daniel Webster

If we and our posterity shall be true to the Christian religion, if we and they shall live always in the fear of God, and shall respect His commandments, if we and they shall maintain just moral sentiments and such conscientious convictions of duty as shall control the heart and life, we may have the highest hopes of the future fortunes of our country . . . But if we and our posterity reject religious institutions and authority, violate the rules of eternal justice, trifle with the injunctions of morality, and recklessly destroy the political constitution which holds us together, no man can tell how sudden a catastrophe may overwhelm us. (February 23, 1852)

Patrick Henry

Patrick Henry further describes the significance of virtue, morality, and religion by noting that all societies and governments receive their strength through this foundation. That when a civil society and its government are based in these principles, then nothing can challenge it and win.

> The great pillars of all government and of social life . . . [are] virtue, morality, and religion. This is the armor, my friend, and this alone that renders us invincible. These are the tactics we should study. If we lose these, we are conquered, fallen indeed. (1799)

David Ramsey, Simeon Howard, and Samuel Cooper

In the following passages, David Ramsey, a delegate to the Continental Congress; Simeon Howard, a pastor who provided his point of view in an election sermon on May 31, 1780; and Reverend Samuel Cooper, a Boston minister who included his thoughts in a sermon on the day of the commencement of the Constitution on October 25, 1780, further confirm the points noted in the previous passages. They confirm that happiness and liberty are rooted in values and character.

David Ramsey

> Remember that there can be no political happiness without liberty; that there can be no liberty without morality; and that there can be no morality without religion. (1789)

Simeon Howard

> The happiness of a people depends greatly upon the character of its rulers. (Massachusetts Election Sermon, May 31, 1780).

Reverend Samuel Cooper

> Virtue is the spirit of a Republic; for where all the power is derived from the people, all depends on their good disposition. (1780)

These historical references provide a starting point for additional exploration and learning. The Founding Generation of the United States provides an exceptional example of the exemplification of strong character. They risked their lives, their families, and their well being to strive to achieve a free and just society. The realization of their vision is a clear demonstration of the power in a strong character rooted in shared values.

Divine Inspiration

Above all else, divine inspiration provides the depth to character development that is required to internalize enduring values. Remember that you are not alone in your journey. You are surrounded by people that love you and will guide you along your way. Most importantly, trust in God. He is always with you.

> The counsel of the Lord stands forever, The plans of His heart to all generations, Blessed is the nation whose God is the Lord, The people He has chosen as His own inheritance. (Ps. 33:10–12)

Parents, you should seek opportunities to explore scripture with your children and discuss the wisdom that God has provided to us. Expanding your family's relationship with God is essential to good character development. The more you come together as a family to examine the knowledge that God has provided to you, the more you will be able to reinforce the lessons your children are pursuing to practice good values and develop their character.

> And these words which I command you today shall be in your heart. You shall teach them diligently to your children, and shall talk of them when you sit in your house, when you walk by the way, when you lie down, and when you rise up. You shall bind them as a sign on your hand, and they shall be as frontlets between your eyes. You shall write them on the doorposts of your house and on your gates. (Deut. 6:6–9)

You must remember to always be learning. This requires constant observation and the openness to incorporate new information into your knowledge base. As a lifelong learner, you will also discover your role as a teacher.

> Only be careful and watch yourselves, closely so that you do not forget the things your eyes have seen or let them fade from your heart as long as you live. Teach them to your children and to their children after them. (Deut. 4:9)

God is a part of everything we do. Let God into your life and you will discover the path to character development. Discovering this path will allow you to turn inward before you act and know what actions you must take that are consistent with your character.

Instructions

The intention of this journal is for each individual to explore his own understanding of each value. Parents, you are the guides. You must be active participants in the process and support your children's progress as they make their way through this journal. Your role is not to provide the answers but to assist your children as they explore their own process to arrive at their unique individual understanding. In order to do this, you will need to structure an approach that works with your schedule.

One approach could be to review one value as a part of your daily routine and reflect on your interpretation of what that value means to you. This should be done early in the day to establish focus on each particular value. The tool provided to aid in this process is the space for you to write your own definition. This will allow you to begin your day by displaying your initial understanding and establishing focus.

You should also review the questions so that as you go through the day, they can be at the forefront of your mind. These questions are designed to allow you to assess your progress of living the daily value and enhance your understanding of the value at the end of each day. These questions are a guide to a deeper understanding of your value. As you reflect on your actions throughout the day, you will be able to personalize each value and internalize the understanding of each value through your personal experience.

The free expression page is there for you to use as you see fit. Please feel free to make notes, draw pictures, write stories, ask your own questions, rewrite your definition, etc.

Above all, remember that this is a lifelong process to define your character. Your experiences will shape who you are. Be prepared to make the most of each day and focus your attention and energy on being the best you that you can be.

Humility

But he who is greatest among you shall be your servant. And whoever exalts himself will be humbled, and he who humbles himself will be exalted.

—Matthew 23:11–12

Humility and the fear of the Lord bring wealth and honor and life.

—Proverbs 22:4

Definition

Date: _ / _ / 20__

Write your own definition. What does humility mean to you?

_____
_____
_____
_____
_____
_____

What challenges did you confront today?

_____
_____
_____
_____

How did you confront those challenges?

_____
_____
_____
_____

What values did you demonstrate when facing those challenges?

_____
_____
_____
_____

How did you challenge yourself today?

_____
_____
_____
_____

How have you lived humility today?

_____
_____
_____
_____

Free Expression

Work

Whatever you do, work at it with all your heart,
as working for the Lord, not for human masters.

—Colossians 3:23

Whatsoever a man soweth,
that shall he also reap.

—Galatians 6:7

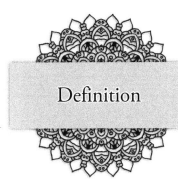

Definition

Date: _ / _ / 20__

Write your own definition. What does work mean to you?

_____

_____

_____

_____

_____

_____

What challenges did you confront today?

How did you confront those challenges?

What values did you demonstrate when facing those challenges?

How did you challenge yourself today?

How have you lived work today?

Free Expression

Discipline /
Self-Discipline

Since an overseer manages God's household
he must be blameless not overbearing, not
quick tempered, not given to drunkenness,
not violent, not pursuing dishonest gain.
Rather he must be hospitable, one who
loves what he does, who is self controlled,
upright, holy and disciplined.
He must hold firmly to the trustworthy
message as it has been taught so that he
can encourage others by sound doctrine
and refute those who oppose it.

—Titus 1:7–9

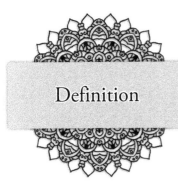

Definition

Date: _ / _ / 20__

Write your own definition. What does discipline mean to you?

_____

_____

_____

_____

_____

_____

What challenges did you confront today?

_____

_____

_____

_____

How did you confront those challenges?

_____

_____

_____

_____

What values did you demonstrate when facing those challenges?

_____

_____

_____

_____

How did you challenge yourself today?

_____

_____

_____

_____

How have you lived discipline today?

_____

_____

_____

_____

Free Expression

Trust

Trust in the Lord with all your heart and
lean not on your own understanding;
in all your ways submit to Him, and
He will make your paths straight.

—Proverbs 3:5–6

God is my refuge and strength, a
very present help in trouble.

—Psalm 46:1

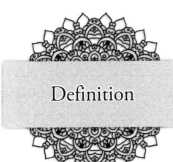

Definition

Date: _ / _ / 20__

Write your own definition. What does trust mean to you?

_____
_____
_____
_____
_____
_____

What challenges did you confront today?

_____

_____

_____

_____

How did you confront those challenges?

_____

_____

_____

_____

What values did you demonstrate when facing those challenges?

_____

_____

_____

_____

How did you challenge yourself today?

_____

_____

_____

_____

How have you lived trust today?

_____

_____

_____

_____

Free Expression

Faith

Now faith is confidence in what we hope for
and assurance about what we do not see.

—Hebrews 11:1

But seek first the kingdom of God
and His righteousness, and all these
things will be given to you.

—Matthew 6:33

Therefore, having been justified by faith, we
have peace with God through our Lord Jesus
Christ, through whom also we have access by
faith into this grace in which we now stand.
And we boast in the hope of the glory of God.

—Romans 5:1–2

The apostles said to the Lord,
"Increase our faith!"
He replied "If you have faith as small
as a mustard seed, you can say to this
mulberry tree, be uprooted and planted
in the sea, and it will obey you."

—Luke 17:5–6

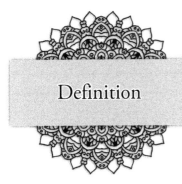

Definition

Date: _ / _ / 20__

Write your own definition. What does faith mean to you?

_____

_____

_____

_____

_____

_____

What challenges did you confront today?

_____

_____

_____

_____

How did you confront those challenges?

_____

_____

_____

_____

What values did you demonstrate when facing those challenges?

_____

_____

_____

_____

How did you challenge yourself today?

_____

_____

_____

_____

How have you lived faith today?

_____

_____

_____

_____

Free Expression

Liberty

Now the Lord is the Spirit; and where the
Spirit of the Lord is, there is Liberty.

—2 Corinthians 3:17

But whoever looks intently into the perfect law
that gives freedom, and continues in it—not
forgetting what they have heard, but doing
it—they will be blessed in what they do.

—James 1:25

So if the Son sets you free, you
will be free indeed.

—John 8:36

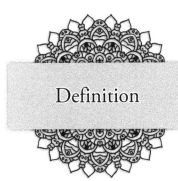

Definition

Date: _ / _ / 20__

Write your own definition. What does liberty mean to you?

_____

_____

_____

_____

_____

_____

What challenges did you confront today?

_____

_____

_____

_____

How did you confront those challenges?

_____

_____

_____

_____

What values did you demonstrate when facing those challenges?

_____

_____

_____

_____

How did you challenge yourself today?

_____

_____

_____

_____

How have you lived liberty today?

_____

_____

_____

_____

Free Expression

Perseverance

Consider it pure joy, my brothers and
sisters, whenever you face trials of many
kinds, because you know that the testing
of your faith produces perseverance.
Let perseverance finish its work so that you may
be mature and complete, not lacking anything.

—James 1:2–4

Therefore, since we are surrounded by
such a great cloud of witnesses, let us
throw off everything that hinders and
the sin that so easily entangles.
And let us run with perseverance
the race marked out for us.

—Hebrews 12:1

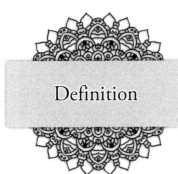

Definition

Date: _ / _ / 20__

Write your own definition. What does perseverance mean to you?

_____
_____
_____
_____
_____
_____

What challenges did you confront today?

_____

_____

_____

_____

How did you confront those challenges?

_____

_____

_____

_____

What values did you demonstrate when facing those challenges?

_____

_____

_____

_____

How did you challenge yourself today?

_____

_____

_____

_____

How have you lived perseverance today?

_____

_____

_____

_____

Free Expression

Love

This is My commandment, that you
love one another as I have loved you.
Greater love has no one than this, than
to lay down one's life for his friends

—John 15:12–13

For you, brethren, have been called to liberty;
only do not use liberty as an opportunity for
the flesh, but through love serve one another.
For all the law is fulfilled in one word, even in
this: "You shall love your neighbor as yourself."

—Galatians 5:13–14

Grant, Lord, that my children may
learn to live a life of love, through
the Spirit who dwells in them.

—Galatians 5:25

A new command I give you: Love
one another. As I have loved you,
so you must love one another.

—John 13:34

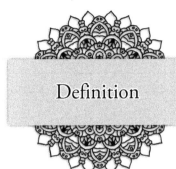

Definition

Write your own definition. What does love mean to you?

_____

_____

_____

_____

_____

_____

What challenges did you confront today?

_____

_____

_____

_____

How did you confront those challenges?

_____

_____

_____

_____

What values did you demonstrate when facing those challenges?

_____

_____

_____

_____

How did you challenge yourself today?

_____

_____

_____

_____

How have you lived love today?

_____

_____

_____

_____

Free Expression

Resilience

Finally be strong in the Lord
and in his mighty power.
Put on the full armor of God so that you can
take your stand against the devil's schemes.
For our struggle is not against flesh and blood,
but against the rulers, against the authorities,
against the powers of this dark world and
against the spiritual forces of evil in heavenly
realms. Therefore, put on the full armor of
God, so that when the day of evil comes,
you may be able to stand your ground, and
after you have done everything, to stand.

—Ephesians 6:10–14

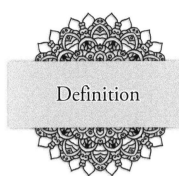

Definition

Date: _ / _ / 20__

Write your own definition. What does resilience mean to you?

_____
_____
_____
_____
_____
_____

What challenges did you confront today?

_____
_____
_____
_____

How did you confront those challenges?

_____
_____
_____
_____

What values did you demonstrate when facing those challenges?

_____
_____
_____
_____

How did you challenge yourself today?

_____
_____
_____
_____

How have you lived resilience today?

_____
_____
_____
_____

Free Expression

Service

Serve whole heartedly, as if you were
serving the Lord, not people.

—Ephesians 6:7

Definition

Date: _ / _ / 20__

Write your own definition. What does service mean to you?

_____

_____

_____

_____

_____

_____

What challenges did you confront today?

_____
_____
_____
_____

How did you confront those challenges?

_____
_____
_____
_____

What values did you demonstrate when facing those challenges?

_____
_____
_____
_____

How did you challenge yourself today?

_____
_____
_____
_____

How have you lived service today?

_____
_____
_____
_____

Free Expression

Prudence

For gaining wisdom and instruction; for understanding words of insight; for receiving instruction in prudent behavior, doing what is right and just and fair; for giving prudence to those who are simple, knowledge and discretion to the young—let the wise listen and add to their learning, and let discerning get guidance—for understanding proverbs and parables the sayings are riddles of the wise.

—Proverbs 1:2–6

A prudent man sees danger and takes refuge, but the simple keep going and suffer for it.

—Proverbs 22:3

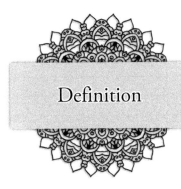

Definition

Date: _ / _ / 20__

Write your own definition. What does prudence mean to you?

_____

_____

_____

_____

_____

_____

What challenges did you confront today?

_____

_____

_____

_____

How did you confront those challenges?

_____

_____

_____

_____

What values did you demonstrate when facing those challenges?

_____

_____

_____

_____

How did you challenge yourself today?

_____

_____

_____

_____

How have you lived prudence today?

_____

_____

_____

_____

Free Expression

Practice
(Deliberate Practice)

Each one should test their own actions. Then
they can take pride in themselves alone,
without comparing themselves to someone
else, for each one should carry their own load.

—Galatians 6:4–5

Definition

Date: _ / _ / 20__

Write your own definition. What does practice mean to you?

_____
_____
_____
_____
_____
_____

What challenges did you confront today?

_____

_____

_____

_____

How did you confront those challenges?

_____

_____

_____

_____

What values did you demonstrate when facing those challenges?

_____

_____

_____

_____

How did you challenge yourself today?

_____

_____

_____

_____

How have you lived practice today?

_____

_____

_____

_____

Free Expression

Courtesy/ Consideration

Remind the people to be subject to rulers and authorities, to be obedient, to be ready to do whatever is good, to slander no one, to be peaceable, and considerate, and always to be gentle toward everyone.

(Titus 3:2).

Definition

Date: _ / _ / 20__

Write your own definition. What does courtesy/consideration mean to you?

_____

_____

_____

_____

_____

_____

What challenges did you confront today?

_____
_____
_____
_____

How did you confront those challenges?

_____
_____
_____
_____

What values did you demonstrate when facing those challenges?

_____
_____
_____
_____

How did you challenge yourself today?

_____
_____
_____
_____

How have you lived courtesy/consideration today?

_____
_____
_____
_____

Free Expression

Gratitude

So, then just as you received Christ
Jesus as Lord, continue to live your lives
in Him, rooted and built up in Him,
strengthened in the faith as you were taught,
and overflowing with thankfulness.

—Colossians 2:6–7

Sing and make music from your heart
to the Lord, always giving thanks to
God the Father for everything, in the
name of our Lord Jesus Christ.

—Ephesians 5:20–21

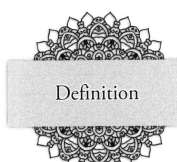

Definition

Date: _ / _ / 20__

Write your own definition. What does gratitude mean to you?

_____

_____

_____

_____

_____

_____

What challenges did you confront today?

_____

_____

_____

_____

How did you confront those challenges?

_____

_____

_____

_____

What values did you demonstrate when facing those challenges?

_____

_____

_____

_____

How did you challenge yourself today?

_____

_____

_____

_____

How have you lived gratitude today?

_____

_____

_____

_____

Free Expression

Respect

Show proper respect to everyone, love the family of believers, fear God, honor the emperor.

—1 Peter 2:17

Children, obey your parents in everything, for this pleases the Lord. Fathers, do not embitter your children, or they will become discouraged.

—Colossians 3:20–21

Definition

Date: _ / _ / 20__

Write your own definition. What does respect mean to you?

_____

_____

_____

_____

_____

_____

What challenges did you confront today?

_____

_____

_____

_____

How did you confront those challenges?

_____

_____

_____

_____

What values did you demonstrate when facing those challenges?

_____

_____

_____

_____

How did you challenge yourself today?

_____

_____

_____

_____

How have you lived respect today?

_____

_____

_____

_____

Free Expression

Concentration/Focus

So then, let us not be like others who are
asleep, but let us be awake and sober.

(1 Thessalonians 5:6).

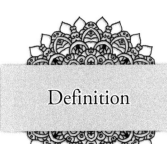

Definition

Date: _ / _ / 20__

Write your own definition. What does concentration / focus mean to you?

_____

_____

_____

_____

_____

_____

What challenges did you confront today?

_____

_____

_____

_____

How did you confront those challenges?

_____

_____

_____

_____

What values did you demonstrate when facing those challenges?

_____

_____

_____

_____

How did you challenge yourself today?

_____

_____

_____

_____

How have you lived concentration/focus today?

_____

_____

_____

_____

Free Expression

Patience

The plans of the diligent lead to profit
as surely as haste leads to poverty.

—Proverbs 21:5

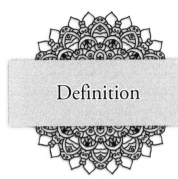

Definition

Date: _ / _ / 20__

Write your own definition. What does patience mean to you?

_____

_____

_____

_____

_____

_____

What challenges did you confront today?

_____

_____

_____

_____

How did you confront those challenges?

_____

_____

_____

_____

What values did you demonstrate when facing those challenges?

_____

_____

_____

_____

How did you challenge yourself today?

_____

_____

_____

_____

How have you lived patience today?

_____

_____

_____

_____

Free Expression

Generosity

The generous will themselves be blessed,
for they share their food with the poor.

—Proverbs 22:9

Command them to do good, to be rich in good
deeds, and to be generous and willing to share.

—1 Timothy 6:18

Whoever is kind to the poor lends
to the Lord, and he will reward
them for what they have done.

—Proverbs 19:17

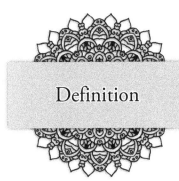

Definition

Date: _ / _ / 20__

Write your own definition. What does generosity mean to you?

_____

_____

_____

_____

_____

_____

What challenges did you confront today?

_____
_____
_____
_____

How did you confront those challenges?

_____
_____
_____
_____

What values did you demonstrate when facing those challenges?

_____
_____
_____
_____

How did you challenge yourself today?

_____
_____
_____
_____

How have you lived generosity today?

_____
_____
_____
_____

Free Expression

Honesty/Integrity

May integrity and uprightness protect
me, because my hope, Lord is in you.

—Psalms 25:21

Definition

Date: _ / _ / 20__

Write your own definition. What do honesty/integrity mean to you?

_____

_____

_____

_____

_____

_____

What challenges did you confront today?

How did you confront those challenges?

What values did you demonstrate when facing those challenges?

How did you challenge yourself today?

How have you lived honesty/integrity today?

Free Expression

Justice

For the Lord is righteous, He loves
justice; the upright will see his face.

—Psalms 11:7

He has shown you, O mortal, what is good.
And what does the Lord require of you?

—Micah 6:8

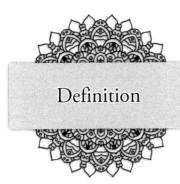

Definition

Date: _ / _ / 20__

Write your own definition. What does justice mean to you?

_____

_____

_____

_____

_____

_____

What challenges did you confront today?

_____
_____
_____
_____

How did you confront those challenges?

_____
_____
_____
_____

What values did you demonstrate when facing those challenges?

_____
_____
_____
_____

How did you challenge yourself today?

_____
_____
_____
_____

How have you lived justice today?

_____
_____
_____
_____

Free Expression

Courage

Be strong and courageous. Do not be afraid or terrified because of them, for the Lord your God goes with you; He will never leave you nor forsake you.

—Deuteronomy 31:6

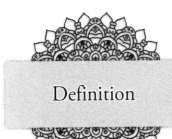

Definition

Date: _ / _ / 20__

Write your own definition. What does courage mean to you?

_____

_____

_____

_____

_____

_____

What challenges did you confront today?

_____

_____

_____

_____

How did you confront those challenges?

_____

_____

_____

_____

What values did you demonstrate when facing those challenges?

_____

_____

_____

_____

How did you challenge yourself today?

_____

_____

_____

_____

How have you lived courage today?

_____

_____

_____

_____

Free Expression

Kindness

Make sure that nobody pays back wrong
for wrong but always strive to do what is
good for each other and everyone else.

—1 Thessalonians 5:15

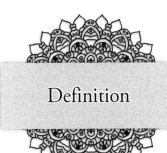

Definition

Date: _ / _ / 20__

Write your own definition. What does kindness mean to you?

_____

_____

_____

_____

_____

_____

What challenges did you confront today?

_____
_____
_____
_____

How did you confront those challenges?

_____
_____
_____
_____

What values did you demonstrate when facing those challenges?

_____
_____
_____
_____

How did you challenge yourself today?

_____
_____
_____
_____

How have you lived kindness today?

_____
_____
_____
_____

Free Expression

Responsibility

Each one should test their own actions. Then
they can take pride in themselves alone,
without comparing themselves to someone
else, for each one should carry their own load.

—Galatians 6:4–5

Train a child in the way he should go, and
when he is old he will not turn from it.

—Proverbs 22:6

Definition

Date: _ / _ / 20__

Write your own definition. What does responsibility mean to you?

_____

_____

_____

_____

_____

_____

What challenges did you confront today?

_____

_____

_____

_____

How did you confront those challenges?

_____

_____

_____

_____

What values did you demonstrate when facing those challenges?

_____

_____

_____

_____

How did you challenge yourself today?

_____

_____

_____

_____

How have you lived responsibility today?

_____

_____

_____

_____

Free Expression

Tolerance

Bear with each other and forgive one another
if any of you has a grievance against someone.
Forgive as the Lord forgave you.

—Colossians 3:13

Definition

Date: _ / _ / 20__

Write your own definition. What does tolerance mean to you?

_____

_____

_____

_____

_____

_____

What challenges did you confront today?

_____

_____

_____

_____

How did you confront those challenges?

_____

_____

_____

_____

What values did you demonstrate when facing those challenges?

_____

_____

_____

_____

How did you challenge yourself today?

_____

_____

_____

_____

How have you lived tolerance today?

_____

_____

_____

_____

Free Expression

Empathy

Whoever shuts their ears to the cry of the
poor will also cry out and not be answered.

—Proverbs 21:13

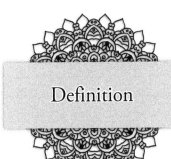

Definition

Date: _ / _ / 20__

Write your own definition. What does empathy mean to you?

_____

_____

_____

_____

_____

_____

What challenges did you confront today?

_____
_____
_____
_____

How did you confront those challenges?

_____
_____
_____
_____

What values did you demonstrate when facing those challenges?

_____
_____
_____
_____

How did you challenge yourself today?

_____
_____
_____
_____

How have you lived empathy today?

_____
_____
_____
_____

Free Expression

Compassion

Though he brings grief, he will show
compassion, so great is his unfailing love.

—Lamentations 3:32

The Lord is gracious and compassionate,
slow to anger and rich in love.
The Lord is good to all; he has
compassion on all he has made.

—Psalm 145:8–9

Praise be to the God and Father of our
Lord Jesus Christ, the Father of compassion
and the God of all comfort, who comforts
us in all our troubles, so that we can
comfort those in any trouble with the
comfort we ourselves receive from God.

—2 Corinthians 1:3–4

Definition

Date: _ / _ / 20__

Write your own definition. What does compassion mean to you?

_____

_____

_____

_____

_____

_____

What challenges did you confront today?

_____

_____

_____

_____

How did you confront those challenges?

_____

_____

_____

_____

What values did you demonstrate when facing those challenges?

_____

_____

_____

_____

How did you challenge yourself today?

_____

_____

_____

_____

How have you lived compassion today?

_____

_____

_____

_____

Free Expression

Loyalty

Let love and faithfulness never leave you; bind them around your neck, write them on the tablet of your heart. Then you will win favor and a good name in the sight of God and man.

—Proverbs 3:3–4

Many claim to have unfailing love, but a faithful person who can find?

—Proverbs 20:6

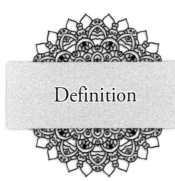

Definition

Date: _ / _ / 20__

Write your own definition. What does loyalty mean to you?

_____

_____

_____

_____

_____

_____

What challenges did you confront today?

_____
_____
_____
_____

How did you confront those challenges?

_____
_____
_____
_____

What values did you demonstrate when facing those challenges?

_____
_____
_____
_____

How did you challenge yourself today?

_____
_____
_____
_____

How have you lived loyalty today?

_____
_____
_____
_____

Free Expression

Friendship

Do not make friends with a hot-tempered man, do not associate with one easily angered, or you may learn his ways and get yourself ensnared.

—Proverbs 22:24–25

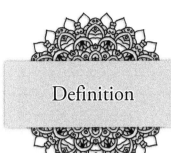

Definition

Date: _ / _ / 20__

Write your own definition. What does friendship mean to you?

_____

_____

_____

_____

_____

_____

What challenges did you confront today?

_____

_____

_____

_____

How did you confront those challenges?

_____

_____

_____

_____

What values did you demonstrate when facing those challenges?

_____

_____

_____

_____

How did you challenge yourself today?

_____

_____

_____

_____

How have you lived friendship today?

_____

_____

_____

_____

Free Expression

Self-Control

Those who want to get rich fall into
temptation and a trap and into many foolish
and harmful desires that plunge people
into ruin and destruction. For the love
of money is a root of all kinds of evil.
Some people, eager for money, have
wandered from the faith and pierced
themselves with many griefs.

—1 Timothy 6:9–10

Fools give full vent to their rage but
the wise bring calm in the end.

—Proverbs 29:11.

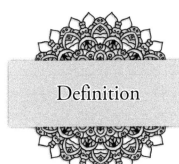

Definition

Date: _ / _ / 20__

Write your own definition. What does self-control mean to you?

_____

_____

_____

_____

_____

_____

What challenges did you confront today?

_____
_____
_____
_____

How did you confront those challenges?

_____
_____
_____
_____

What values did you demonstrate when facing those challenges?

_____
_____
_____
_____

How did you challenge yourself today?

_____
_____
_____
_____

How have you lived self-control today?

_____
_____
_____
_____

Free Expression

Mercy

When the kindness and love of God our Savior appeared He saved us, not because of righteous things we had done, but because of his mercy.

—Titus 3:4–5

Speak and act as those who are going to be judged by the law that gives freedom, because judgement without mercy will be shown to anyone who has not been merciful. Mercy triumphs over judgement.

—James 2:12–15

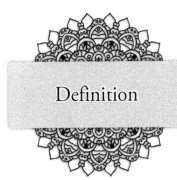

Definition

Date: _ / _ / 20__

Write your own definition. What does mercy mean to you?

_____

_____

_____

_____

_____

_____

What challenges did you confront today?

_____

_____

_____

_____

How did you confront those challenges?

_____

_____

_____

_____

What values did you demonstrate when facing those challenges?

_____

_____

_____

_____

How did you challenge yourself today?

_____

_____

_____

_____

How have you lived mercy today?

_____

_____

_____

_____

Free Expression

Contentedness

But godliness with contentment is great gain. For we brought nothing into the world, and we can take nothing out of it. But if we have food and clothing, we will be content with that.

—1 Timothy 6:6–8

Definition

Date: _ / _ / 20__

Write your own definition. What does contentedness mean to you?

_____

_____

_____

_____

_____

_____

What challenges did you confront today?

_____
_____
_____
_____

How did you confront those challenges?

_____
_____
_____
_____

What values did you demonstrate when facing those challenges?

_____
_____
_____
_____

How did you challenge yourself today?

_____
_____
_____
_____

How have you lived contentedness today?

_____
_____
_____
_____

Free Expression

About the Author

Steven Johnson is a husband and father of two beautiful children, a son and a daughter. He has spent over eighteen years working for the Department of Defense in various capacities, including nearly nine years in the army conducting psychological operations in Peru, Colombia, and Iraq, and nine years in a civilian capacity working at the strategic command level. His time in the army was exclusively spent in special operations, which represents a close-knit community driven by a strong devotion to shared values.

Steven has a bachelor of arts in business administrations and a master's of science in international relations and conflict resolution. His master's studies involved gaining an in-depth understanding of intersocietal conflict dynamics and resolutions that ultimately lead to mutual acceptance. Steven uses the skills gained from his academic studies to continue to support US efforts to resolve complex situations all over the world.

Steven's experience and education have allowed him to personally explore the benefits and shortfalls of values in diverse societies around the globe. This has led him to believe that the foundation of any society requires vigilant character development.

CPSIA information can be obtained
at www.ICGtesting.com
Printed in the USA
BVHW072042171218
535790BV00011B/862/P